How to Sing to a Dago

Essential Poets Series 69

Rachel Guido deVries

How to Sing to a Dago
and Other Canzonetti

Guernica
Toronto / New York
1996

Copyright © 1996 Rachel Guido deVries and Guernica Editions Inc.
All rights reserved.
Printed in Canada.

Antonio D'Alfonso, editor.
Guernica Editions Inc.
P. O. Box 117, Station P, Toronto (ON), Canada M5S 2S6
340 Nagel Drive, Cheektowaga, N.Y. 14225-4731 U.S.A.

Legal Deposit — Second Quarter
National Library of Canada.
Library of Congress Catalog Card Number: 94-74386

Canadian Cataloguing in Publication Data
deVries, Rachel Guido, 1947-
How to sing to a Dago, and other canzonetti
(Essential poets series ; 69)
Poems.
ISBN 1-55071-028-1
I. Title. II. Series.
PS3554.E9284H69   1996   811'.54   C94-900882-6

Contents

How to Sing to a Dago

A Stone, A Ruby, The Sea 11
Mamma 13
Aunt Jo 14
Italian Grocer 15
On Alabama Ave., Paterson, 1954 16
Toothache 17
Step on a Crack 18
Litany on the Equinox 19
I Dream a Dish of Seashell 21
Blood Dreamer 23
Feather/Scale/Egg 25
Anniversary 26
How to Sing to a Dago 27
Bluedaddy's Side of the Story 29
Elena in a Sea of Dreams 31

The Notmother Songs

Before Dawn, Before Thanksgiving the
    Notmother Visits 35
Ifs for the Notmother from Paterson 38
Sea Stones 40
Coastal Travelling 42
You Again, with Double-Headed Cobra 44
After 45
Spoken from the Calabash: Shimoni, Kenya 48
Hands Like Birds, Flying 51

Daydream/Soon 53
Blues Bird/Darling Bird 54
First Desire/First Time 55
Full of Desire, Dreaming 56
Little Fires 57
Blue 58
Wild 59
Dance Alone in a Bare Room 60

Birds, Remembering

Birds of Sorrow 63
Bird of Silence 64
Silly Bird, I Love You 65
Hot Bird of Longing 66
Crying Bird 67
Bird of the Lake 68

Acknowledgments

Some of these poems have been published in the following publications: Birds, Remembering: "Frontiers, A Journal of Women's Studies"; Blood Dreamer: "Voices in Italian America"; Litany on the Equinox: "Sinister Wisdom" and "la bella figura"; Step on a Crack: *An Arc of Light;* After: "Ikon"; Hands Like Birds, Flying, Daydream / Soon, Blues Bird / Darling Bird, First Desire / First Time, Full of Desire, Dreaming, Little Fires, Blue, Wild: "Yellow Silk"; Italian Grocer, Toothache, On Alabama Avenue, Paterson, 1954: "Voices in Italian Americana"; Anniversary: "One Fell Swoop."

All lines from *The Calculus of Variation* are from Diane di Prima's book of the same title.

for Diane di Prima

How to Sing
to a Dago

A Stone, A Ruby, The Sea

Beginning in you
Marietta Guido
Daughter of
Rachel Martini
Sister of
Mary
Josephine
Angelina
Rita
Irene
Mother of
Rachel
Rita
John
Grandmother of
Lorri

I come
from centuries
of Calabrese women
heads hard as stone
I am
shaped by Calabrese women
who breathed near the sea
who are in me
what is in me
What I am
a ruby in stone
or a Rubanesque ruby
in my Mamma's mind

From a cave
near the sea
where my mothers danced
Cave I call
dream or *song*
the cave of cavorting
the cave of stone

Stone as metaphor
Stone as a lover, once
Stone as a place to sharpen
my teeth, my wits, my tongue
my tongue   my tongue

There is a sea
of women
glistening like stones
caressed by the sea
I am a woman like a ruby
in this sea

Mamma

laughter bell-like
your slender leg
sloping on the bed
gently   and alone

blue nightie caressing
knees   hand tucked up
beneath your chin   so
lovely I weep recalling

Aunt Jo

with a shot of whiskey
and a bowling ball
A brassy voice
and a fierce fierce
mouth   the one
they say I follow

you showed me
love inside the argument
the fieriness
of belief
and how to share
a Hershey bar with almonds
a steak sandwich
a sapphire
one September

Italian Grocer

After he was produce manager for the A & P,
Pop opened his own store. He polished apples
to lay alongside sweet Jersey peaches all
fuzzy and gold, and sometimes got figs which he
held up like gems. Bread and baccala, olives
in a big brown barrel. Provolone, locatelli,
Genoa salami, prosciutto behind a gleaming
case. Each morning he donned a white coat
like a doctor, marched the aisles, and watched.

He hired Angie the dyke to keep things neat.
She fed me cherries when I was three. Mamma
worried I'd choke. Pop and Angie laughed
and Angie said I'd learn what to do
with those pits.

When the store burned, Pop went mad and wept
all over the street. Angie vanished from me, and
the queer man upstairs lost all of his drag. White
people in the neighborhood said Pop the Wop
torched his own store for insurance. He had none.
His white coat, smelling of cheese and fish,
was gone.

On Alabama Ave., Paterson, 1954

At seven I dreamed again and again
of plummeting down the narrow stairs
into the arms of Mario the greenhorn
with his curly black hair. Old
Mrs. Pepe cleaned scungilli outside
on the porch. I watched her big hands
go in and out of the pot and thought
about her son Mario wishing he were
my pop. In the tiny flat on the third
floor, Pop was already bald and bellowing
rage. Mamma bit her tongue into silence
she never stopped wishing on me.

When Mamma's five sisters came over
she was happy. They talked dirty
in Calabrian and laughed loud. They
smacked each other on the back or
grabbed hands, smoked cigarets and
ate the whole time, coffee cake, macaroni,
meatballs, biscotti, and fruit. Little
apricots sweet and delicate and yellow,
and tossed the smooth brown pits
on a blue plate, where they clattered
like dice.

Toothache

When Pop was in jail, Mamma
swept and swept the stairs, ate
sardines with raw onions, and
rose at five each morning
to open the store, put out
the newspapers, fry eggs
and Taylor ham, restock
the candy and gum. She
kept answering his bookie's
phone and ran messages to Pop
each night in his cell. I
was ashamed and avoided them both.
I offered no help. I had
a toothache for weeks I ignored
and finally let a quack dentist
with a dirty office, right down
the street from the store, yank
out two molars. Then I stuffed
my mouth with gauze.

Step on a Crack

> *Step on a crack*
> *you'll break your mother's back.*
> *Step on a line*
> *you'll break your mother's spine.*

All my life I've tried to obey
that rhyme, leaping across sidewalks
to ensure your safety.
Now the lines grow thicker,
and weeds sprout in the cracks.
They are harder to avoid.
Your voice is turning shrill
and your temper short and feisty.
My brother tells me, with horror,
that you've taken to using foul language.
I am sick with guilt
for all the times I must have slipped
so my foot touched the line,
sending enemy soldiers up and down your back.
They've laid mines across your synapses
and sabotaged the guards in your brain.
They loom like spies in your eyes.
You stay home, drawing the curtains
and praying in Italian.
I am here, powerless and sorry,
drawing lines with great chinks in them,
filling the spaces with memories.

Litany on the Equinox

The Earth is my mother
she maketh me in her image
I shall always want
her voice   wind through trees
in fall   rush of waves
at midnight or dawn
the earth dark as the lover
I dream of on the eve
of the equinox   big breasted
woman, mountains rosy tipped
as sunrise above the hills
and streams of my body
The earth is my mother
she maketh me in her image
I shall always want
her storms raging
her volcanos' roiling
the eyes of her hurricanes
her tornadoes' warnings
her center deeper
than any canyon
or black hole shows
The earth is my mother
she maketh me in her image
I shall always want
her stars, her moons, her suns,
her galaxies, her universe
I shall be a star floating
through heaven ready to burst

new light
The earth is my mother
she maketh me in her image
I shall always want
her gorges for my own
her waterfalls, her whirlpools,
her underground caves, her sea caves
where the light is blue
and she waits in a shape
of anemone or gnome
where she speaks
in many tongues
I want as my own
The earth is my mother
I am made in her image
bones like trees, flesh
like clay, blood like rivers,
sex like the ocean
eyes that burn in the center
of wanting to be
The earth
is my mother
I am made in her image
and I
shall
always
want

I Dream a Dish of Seashell

You
you
you
entered
the door opened
the dreams begin
You give me a dish
you made
from stuff of sea
a dish of shell
ancient   crumbling a little
ancient   the smell
of seaweed   whorled
with memory   your
name etched in its
old old surface
like a rune
I start to decipher
through the undertow
high tide full of passion
and rage and love
full of revolutions
the sea's turning
and turning through
centuries   the blue
water near Sicily
only in dreams
the voices echoing
through the seadish

you made me
call me back
again home is the sea
where the heart
can rise and fall
and in my dream
the blue hope
fills me   I wake
for the first time
in months having
slept all night
In the cool spring morning
the scent of ocean
in my bed of beach roses
the feel of waves
rippling through all of me
your name on a dish
like an ancient rune
I could spend all my lifetimes
deciphering

Blood Dreamer

I

Dog at her side, breasts heavy with love
she leans, and fills the fire with sorrow,

soft ashes make at first a comforting sound
as she moves them, the stick poking, poking

until an ember catches the stick. For a moment
the light is heavy, orange, like a sunset's

flame along the beach. Lovers' tongues, like
little fires, a memory, as though she is old

the dog's muzzle is gray, she lounges
with her ankles crossed on the grass, the lap-

lap of the water makes a heavy sound along
the slatted pier she can see

from the mouth of the cave   at moonlight
she raises her legs, blood passes, small

river without love and red with dreaming
like the sunrise at lakeside   the last morning

she appeared.

II

Sugar tooth, craving for a sweet tit
end of the cycle, belly flat again

and it begins, the yearning, slow ache
like a toothache, like something big

at the top of a hill, just beginning
to consider rolling all over again

and grass like cilia waves, a small
symphony of waves and blue music, while

all the time a slow roll of pleasure
like the winging of another span

and you could die laughing in it, the whole
time sucking on your sweet tooth while

your breasts swell, a little wave, like farewell
or like a welcome

Feather/Scale/Egg

Old feather floating downstream
from the time the sky opened:
blue notes, white feathers
and so many stones slippery with moss.

Skipping stones: one two three
leaps of the flat-bellied stones
on their way across the lake
or they sink fast, like stones, to the deep.

A fish, a bird: scales and feathers
all shiny with light. Blood
courses through my belly on its way out.
An egg falls, into the center of the dark

from either side the fish, the bird, and I
have a wild eye and eggs gleaming with love.
The notmother unties hope
from the burning stake. Shh. Hear the moan:

It is the fire burning, the wing
of a bird slicing through blue air,
the fish finning toward sea,
or me, opening to the losses.

Anniversary

for Mamma

Never mind the moments when the sky goes dark
with his refusal to speak. Never mind
the sound of his saw whirring down cellar
all evening. Upstairs you stir the gravy,
whisper a novena and finger beads while
the kitchen grows warm with your feeling.
All the time you're thinking this is what
it comes to: the buzzing of the blade
in the damp and musty insides of the house,
a place of silence and no mystery. When
you run out of beads on the rosary your
patience snaps like a bone bent backward,
the angle at last unnatural. His steps
up the stairs sound ridiculous, stubborn
as stone. He pokes his way toward
the kitchen and you see how his bald head
has a dull sheen, like a candled egg,
and you go with your wooden spoon crack
crack on the stove top, imagining.

How to Sing to a Dago

> Wop wop wop, wop wop a guinea guinea,
> Wop wop wop, wop wop a guinea guinea
> all day, all day, as the dagos on

I mean I can laugh at myself, greaseball
that I am with a bumpy nose and a mouth
full of garlic. Hardy har har you all know
how the ginzo can laugh up a storm and how she
loves to get laid. Put your tongue inside me,
I'm a putana, give me spaghetti with bacon,
one big wooden spoon and I'll be happy
with my shoes off and no babe in the room.

> Wop wop wop, wop wop a guinea guinea,
> Wop wop wop, wop wop a guinea guinea
> all day, all day, as the dagos on

When I'm quiet I'm thinking, a surprise to you
all, but my voice is like thunder inside of
a storm. I listen to voices that tell me to hush
but I'm hungry for music, in love with all touch.
What I want is more feeling, what I want is too much
for the white girls who tell me Italians are loud
and the others who say they will not take me out,
I might yell in a fury or scream in my joy.
That makes them feel funny, ashamed of their choice.

> Wop wop wop, wop wop a guinea guinea,
> Wop wop wop, wop wop a guinea guinea
> all day, all day, as the dagos on

When you sing to this dago my ears come to life
and it don't matter if the words aren't perfect
or nice. What matters is singing at the top
of your voice and then being ready to listen
to mine. When I lay my mouth to your ear,
my tongue in its shell, I'm singing a love
song and singing it well:

> Wop wop wop, wop wop a guinea guinea,
> Wop wop wop, wop wop a guinea guinea
> all day, all day, as the dagos on

Bluedaddy's Side of the Story

Bluedaddy is sad because he never
gets what he wants, needs. He stood

back from the crowds and watched millionaires
twirl ribbons beneath a startlingly blue

sky, fluttering their fingers in air they
were the guards of, their thin smiling

lips full of lies Bluedaddy saw. Later, he
twisted the truth too, to relax, who could

blame him? His fingers were twisted
and sore, full of little grease burns

and the old lady only believed
in the body. Near the blue sea

she held fire in her hands, knew when
to use it. Sometimes she filled up

with sorrow for Bluedaddy, who thought
being good was an answer.

She has a wicked sense of humor, she loves
her toes and breasts, she moves

when she wants to, almost gliding
through time. It doesn't make much difference

to her who twirls ribbons in front of what crowds.
But she's so old, it's easy to see why

and all of her children are trees now. She
loves how they get to witness

the earth. Wiggling their roots in the ground
she can feel in her feet. Blinking

her eyes full of stars, because night
sky has always been her favorite.

But poor Bluedaddy with his short legs
and short short neck. They could have saved

him from sweeping, hanging. He's the one
who wanted babies

to save him from losing. He never dreamed
they never lasted, or that they changed.

She still tends him, the sweetest ways.
Brushing his soft white hair away

from his eyes. He knows this. They love
coffee, dipping hard bread and butter, their birds.

See? The simplest talk. Don't make
it harder. Listen to the cracking trees,

notice how greens grow best in cool weather.
Think of beans, too, some more bread

for sopping up the juice. As close to the earth
as you'll ever get, Bluedaddy, still breathing.

Elena in a Sea of Dreams

I

The daughter sleeps. Light is curled up
in her small fists, little rivers of light
she reveals in my dreams. Little rivers,
little light, little Elena sleeps each night
when I wander sometimes trembling. Each
time I hold a child in my arms, my only arms,
like infants I used to kiss. The slope
of my upper arm, its pliant flesh, the tender
place where babies lay their heads. What I am
so motherly unyielding and vulnerable to love,
sorrow like a blue curtain swaying in afternoon
light, a little laugh always waiting in the back
of my throat. Who I call notmother begins singing
my name. The red bird finagles on her shoulder
for her ear. But she's mine now, living inside me,

the beginning of swimming and I like it. I welcome
Elena's small rivers, blue lights reflecting, waves
meandering along the shore. *Tiptoe, tiptoe
beneath the twinkling stars*

                stars open in Elena's fists,
her palms bloom with stars yellow and blue. One hundred
years ago and they still became orphans. I name them
orphans of mine, the freckles on my shoulders,
the shifting sweet tune of a flute

II

At thirteen Elena is willowy and filled with rage.
I dream of Sicily, the old woman gnarled with sorrow
and loss, her man-like hands. When her father dies
at last she is seventy, *mala femmina,* so sorely
used. She holds a bowl of fire in her hands,
burns it till he is no longer known. The icy
sill only then receives the bowl

Hiss. Psst. There's a mystery, a rhythm to all
this. Birth and death. Snake eyes, wild eyes,
the eyes of all the birds sliding with time
right into my chest, solar plexus, a nexus of stars.
Elena sometimes wails there so full of stars
it hurts me. Later it'll be howling she yells,
its glory. Morning is her playful time. She
makes me laugh, the little demon.

III

Long ago:

      the last time
the moon was holy
it was in a small girl's curled
fist. Light streamed through
in ribbons, in puffs of smoke.
Beneath her water hyacinths at first
were startling. So purple. They
bloomed right on the surface of green
water, a little pond, very close to the sea:

    'It was me,' Elena whispers, before waking.

The Notmother Songs

Before Dawn, Before Thanksgiving,
The Notmother Visits

> *...like a poem in the dark – escaped back*
>   *to oblivion*
> *No more to say, and nothing to weep for*
> *but the Beings in the Dream*
>
> Allen Ginsberg, 'Kaddish,'
> in *Collected Poems*, p. 209

I know this shallow
light, how it goes
out slow and lovely still
trapped by its own disappearing,
its memory
        vanished

the family I believe
I once knew, the young
boy I married, common
birds I love, mammas
and sisters, their
seventeen girls, that
plump time of girltalk
a thing gone all flat

        Later
say reverence of the body
along the lines of love

        to say
reverence of the body along the lines
of love, the physical planes, my

occasional bliss.
Peaceful tables red candles
gentle and slow:
That dream he once told me
is all in your head

      Beings of Dreams
keep me edgy all night they
prance or call or I flirt
like that, I love to flirt
all night, desire, the peril
a solitary wing
                covered by sky
                it could become
the rim of this wall: Oh, help
yrself over, stop naming it
dream. Screaming still
in the night are the Dreamers,
their Queen, one's for freedom
and pleasure, all wild with sin.
Small gossips, tender ears shelly
pink in the dawn. Two keep a hold
of fear, small though it is,
in the bowl of their hands.
They will share it or hoard it
a cell of despair perhaps lovely
as lace all see through and
fine. Laugh, remember sunlight,
the key, the keyhole through
which she says sotto voce
some souls still emerge
sometimes smiling.

Remember, she says, to bow your head
as though grateful, to cup your hands
as though praying
for nothing but light to call
your fingers home

Ifs for the Notmother from Paterson

Already large and prone to swell
mid-cycle when the birds' harping
at the window made an insane sound
in your heart   like spring
the greening or never like winter.
At the moment of giving up maybe
there was the sound of ocean, heartbeat
& later in the blackness, when your
swirling sought stars, only stars
in the heavy blue sky you swept
the galaxy like a used-to-be
broom on linoleum
And a hardy-har laugh to you too
for that one   what used to be
broom, notmother, big knockers
and that so round belly,
not, after all, a mound of sorrow
behind you

The silk mills closed before
I was born, the key was missing
from the sunlight   I got lost
in the limbo I saw like bodiless
heads in blue sky   the torsos
of pleasure below where sin lived
and heaven where the rich rose
to the tops of clouds, like a hilltop,
and gleamed out through yellow shutters
at the incompletes

so my sentences will always dangle
remain unfinished   the leftover
sound just floating in the air
between dreamers   One day I open
an old book and a song starts
late at night in the same language
I never heard before   My heart
burns like my clit with the desire,
just the desire.

Sea Stones

> *The kind you pick up and stick*
> *in your pocket, not thinking once*
> *why it was they were lying there at all.*
>
> P. E. McGrath, *Provincetown*

Nothing could measure the first circling
The gulls were so random   never settling
for the small part of sea just beyond
our kitchen window   We hovered at the table
singing melancholy tunes of love lost
but really it was passion's turning
to calm that alarmed us

Once in July we laughed all day on the beach
Your freckles began to appear   and I
squirmed all over the blanket noticing a shift in air:
time   its motion and the way we knew something reckless
in us had changed forever

The moon came full four times   magic
number half of your luck   and I
was turning the color of a penny over
and over in my hands   Prayer and sacrifice
in the sand and sea stones we collected
seeking one that would yield to light

August   Psilocybin and the ocean's
shimmer at low tide   so much life and
the hermit crabs skittering with their homes intact
You moved into melancholy twilight full of recognition
and light so tender my heart ached watching

That night the last full circle anchored in the sky
like a perfect stone: 'Harvest Moon,' you said,
gazing upward.

Coastal Traveling

Silence, so long, the night stops.
Morning opens, a tiny tiny bird
flutters near the edge of sleep,
chirps soft against my ear:
Swim   Swim as though your life

depended on it

as though sleep
were a raft for floating,
as though time
were a red and white beach-ball
bobbing to the sea's gentler
rhythm, as though you could
choose a direction, follow it,
swimming sleek as a seal
stopping only to sun

to bask on a rock along
a foreign coast, where the heat
is so familiar you lie defenseless
and brave   Later, catch
fish or listen to the clams'
whisssh against water, later
lie by the fire's edge,
a lover's tongue caressing
your sleek and sunny body
salty, glowing like a pearl
in the sand at moonlight:

Settle for dreaming, ear
pressed to conch shell, heart
against sand at the edge, at
the very edge of the sea.

You Again, with Double-Headed Cobra

> *And then I arrived at the powerful green hill.*
> Muriel Rukeyser,
> *'Then I Saw What the Calling Was'*

It's you again, charmer of snakes from a distant
place where I dream in your lap, throne of power,
mountain like a daughter of earth, round and green.
Around your shoulders lies a double-headed cobra
that I am at first terrified to touch. Then
it raises its two mouths and smiles. You
fade away like the mist each morning, leaving
the snake in place of your heartbeat, rhythm
of sea and blue power. Eels swim wildly alongside
the fish that fly into birds soaring over caves.
The cobra sees too and begins its return.
I follow dancing and spinning as long as I can.
A window bangs shut on the eye I yearn for, waking.
I walk to the meadow alone at sunrise, reaching my arms
toward the heaven like the sea. I see a small opening,
the mouth of a cave. The cobra slides to my waist
where it sparkles in light, turning its double heads
as if searching. When I open my mouth
I speak with triple tongues. My heartbeat echoes
the sound of a drum from the powerful mountain.

After

for P. E. M.

*she ate dried apricots. third suicide era.
after a certain point all the colors are muddy.*
The Calculus of Variation

Lost friend, lover, wing of a bird:
you float downstream, a paper boat,
white, snow all winter and alone
the fire burned, the base you
created/destroyed like all the dollars
that could have brought you
fluttering
        home

Months after silence you call:
  now your father has Alzheimer's
or some drunkenness has settled
in the smoke of his brain,
gray matter like a cloud, ephemeral,
full of poison and stones

All those stones we threw back into
the sea the summer our love
caught on, and off: you grew
sunburned and thin and surly
and I grew old and a little afraid

of you: that reckless edge
of danger for its own sake only,
even the sexual tremor gone,
only the ache it provoked,

a need like a burning in our bellies
for more, to ride white surf alone or
entwined with a lover in a small blue
boat as waves rocked and took us away

that night, with the mirror balanced
on our knees, the mushrooms making
our vision huge, we saw many things
from the deck of our house:
a fat moon rollicking in a deep blue
sky, white topped waves heaving up to reach it,
a skunk at the door we mistook for a cat, the familiar
call of love: another woman's heart
you tried to yank into your mouth, and left me,
alone, with my pulse racing every time I lay down
till you returned at 4 A.M. I could have
cried for your breaking there like a girl,
but the tide was already pulling you
back/the candle's fire, what we had made
home – the circle between us, white with
light and only ours, no longer enough
or too much

Your lover does needles in a brownstone
in Brooklyn like a million others
and you find it unique, the final
dare, a shoot of the silver dice you used
to carry till you lost them somewhere
in a white-out a final time in upstate
or was it in Provincetown that night our
last friend fell face down and smashed
the mirror: we all laughed, cruel with
late-August, each of us close to the edge

of dancing or falling away, eyes glassy
with fear or madness, the mirror's shards
gleaming around her, arrow-shaped, her ragged
sigh

Thirteen years ago I dreamt these images: you
as a knight, white horse mistaken for safety
and you carried me off to garden or cliff, we
had to choose. The hoofs of your horse made
a bright clean sound as you galloped away. The sky
darkened with evening and I stayed alone, waiting.
You are vanishing now, like your father's memory,
while you sit all alone waiting too,
for something to save you, not the white horse,
never a knight. I try to dream something else:
you with your pale hands in the ground this May
as it warms and opens, your head resting on a soft
belly of earth, ears full of seeds and voices,
your arms loose and growing sunburned, your
face like that moon we'll remember as we eat fruit
in my garden, tossing the stones past the snow fence,
listening to the woodpecker busy with home, the sparrow
brave and so small in the fiery sky, the muddy creek
running fast behind the house, and, becoming
distant, the sound of the horse taking leave.

Spoken from the Calabash: Shimoni, Kenya

※

Can be sounds of fear
turbulent, moving in a spiral, a dream
state when the body immobilizes.
Mothers, friends, beckon   appear
sinister   misshapen

It takes days to survive
remembering   remembering   and urging
the present clean   Backyard journeys
clutter the cave and a motion
hurts   like an ache on the will
sad for itself   nostalgia for a world
I can't live in

Forward, backward, around around
little wings, the tiny bird
near my heart, the fluttering
triumphs of flight   The rest
the heart needs to discover

In a moment I could turn to water
float there or uncover a mystery
a dream of the universe

the gulls call   This is today

❧

A feeling all in colors   the drawing
comes like a poem
perfect eyes lips   find themselves
in something known   so old
so old   like the flute's perfect pitch
at sunrise   This is the color the sound
a landing site to live for

❧

Sometimes I hear voices I listen
they say   *turn left*
they say   *the heart the mirror*
the eyes

❧

There were four spirits in the calabash
in Shimoni, in Kenya   Three were out walking
I had to wait for their return
pay respect   and listen, I heard
soft voices   I was *Kali* they said
kali sana   very fierce   and oh yes
I trembled

Kali   the will the hunger is keen
Kali sana   as the tree stretches to sky
and roots so deeply in the earth

❧

I land for days in the world   Get drunk
make love   Everything lives in the body then
everything becomes   not real as the spinning
dreams that leave me   the knowledge
they bring   the imagination the body knows
better than lust or the soft inside of a woman

❧

It is me, me   the hunger
the edge of morning's delicate mouth
pink and seductive   The light of candle
in day the texture of sand   The life in parts
the way I fall in love part by part and say the oh
of bliss round and pliant

❧

I awaken only in the cave   discovering
harmonies   Sung in the universe they move
with air a melody of air dark harmonies
the light   and so few syllables

Hands Like Birds, Flying

Five a.m.
I wake/with you
in my hands
wet/ready
to take you
in my hands
like birds
flying
Two hands
I hold up
and flutter
slow until
all I desire
becomes a love song
filling the air
with blue
Yesterday
a heron
flew by
you ran to feed it
              poised like that
at the edge of the lake
in gray sky and your
so trusting play
fullness And later still
blue sheets turned down
it was raining and Sunday
at dusk and you loved me
again   like always

softly laughing/yr hands
slow in motion/yr hands
like birds flying
inside me

Daydream/Soon

Moaning and laughing like the sea
soon I will sprawl alongside you.
At last, I'll sigh, beneath my fierce
desire to believe your face.
I want your wild hair along
my breasts, your legs slowly dancing
to thigh and the place you soften
ablaze. Longing is lovely from
miles away. I recall your
mouth, its thrill delighting my throat,
I know a little of roaming
my hands along your shoulders all
freckled with gold. Here we laugh loud
like the waves. Gulls' call. We're all full
of pleasure. Oh baby, come soon.

Blues Bird/Darling Bird

Sunset at a calm lake. Old memories, wild times,
all I have lost along the way. Bird of sorrow,
silly bird, crying bird. Small deaths
approach, certain as midnight. Alone late
evening voices like ghosts begin collecting
at the table in the candle's glow, the peaceful
music, the sadness. My desire goes wild for you.
But you are far from me, a memory I covet
and hoard in big hunger. You are more
than I expected, the low moan in my throat
is dying for your ears, for your thighs around
me, your hands along the shoulder I tilt your way
in dreams all day in the rain and the fog. I
want to feel your wetness on my face
and in my hands. I want to press myself close
to you. Small birds skitter along the lake's calm
green surface. Occasionally a gull's call fills
me with trembling. I want you at my lover's house,
irrational, full of desire blazing with those stars
again and still near the still waters of this little
lake, the way I go so wet just imagining you. Longing
is lovely is my refrain, the trills of birds, even
the buzz of airplane in sky. Like the river merchant's
wife, I pine for you, my lovergirl, shy woman
in flames. You fly at night through dreams,
in morning I'm all full of sadness. The blues,
a song I can't stop hearing way down in my throat,
swelling with longing.

First Desire/First Time

again. The Hudson begins its watery curve.
Lay low. I tremble with longing. Maple and aspen
along the shoreline tremble too, leaves all silvery
at seven. I fill up with juice for the life of it.
The green of me stretches, lithe, a sapling. I
long for you. Though I've not yet touched you
taste bone sweet, your scent is in my sleep. I wake
wet and hungry, my mouth a dream between your thighs.
The river runs fierce just here. In its reflection
trees rustle and lean, ablaze.

Full of Desire, Dreaming

Out of the deep side of a dream
love appears, the messenger odd
again. My aunt, long dead,
appears in a mall, wildly
waving at me, though my hair
has thinned and my mother,
once more, is pregnant.

I wake wet with lust
for a stranger. Next
day I ride the train
her way and meet
an Italian like my aunt.
A nervous sort, afraid
to smoke or pee alone.
She clings to me.

I know these are signs
of love. It's spring.
The buds are out. Sex
and death and love along
the Hudson. I'm
hot for you. I ride
the train alone,
full of desire,
dreaming.

Little Fires

Come on. I want to climb your body like a tree,
rest beneath your big breasts, slide my mouth
slow like a fish floating in a lake. I can
dart my tongue like a silver minnow all shiny
with stars inside you. Along the last curve,
where the hottest darkness is, I'll leave
a single star for later. Hours after I
re-enter the sky, you'll know its silvery
feel. Watch for the moon to rise,
for its companions to fill the night. I want
to fill you up like that, hot stars dancing
on my tongue like little fires I burn inside you.

Blue

I touch the blue throat of a tamarack tree
because I believe it might curve right into
the hot eye of a woman I desire. I kiss
the soft leaves lingering so long careful
not to bruise them. The air slides a cloud
into longing.

Later I rest on a rock. The air has cooled.
The sharp neck of desire loosens my throat,
wavers, then returns. The tamarack tree
moves near the sea. Its blue throat astonishes
me. It's the blue eye of fire. It's the woman
I desire.

Wild

late at night a bird croons. Next door
the neighbor bangs into dark. I lay
alone watching stars appear and dream
of love again, its soft center, my desire

always fills the air with madness
especially in spring at midnight.
The iris begins its urgent press against
the bedroom's wall. The sound of love

is rushing in the creek. Out back
my old dog's spirit calls for a stroll,
stars keep appearing, brighter and brighter,
almost harsh with their gleaming, and you

my secret, only a dream, are wild
and sparkle where the minnows run,
flushed by the moon. I swim and swim
all night, in dark and silky water.

Dance Alone in a Bare Room

My calves, milky white from a long winter,
are the first to know time. Later
they'll ache with the joy of it, and
solitude's slow way home will remember
little else. Sun streams through the south
window, late afternoon, my dulcimer hangs
alone near an old rough beam. In a corner
fronds of palm sway as though in summer's
breeze, lazy, like the cats who linger
along the sill.

But still, I'm watching the motion
as though I'm dreaming, sound/asleep after
prowling around at 3 A.M., seeking
silence. Tiny light flickers near the bed:
moonlight waltzing through the skylights.
My lover's shoulder, the small hill
it relates, the golden sheen of moon
along her arm. Sometimes, time
is delicate, a little flower, worth
staying up for.

And then it's broad daylight. I'm
home dreaming of dancing but I can't
lose the duet. First, I read the letter,
then I slide to the poem. The day
is like a horse all at once breaking
into sound full gallop. Its back's all
shiny with sweat, its legs begin to ache
until the sun, at last, goes down, when
it kicks up its heels and dances, alone,
full of moonlight.

Birds, Remembering

They do not use the stairs, the spirits of your ancestors.
The Calculus of Variation

Birds of Sorrow

They don't fly in the window either, bad luck
that could bring. They don't come down
the chimney, no fluttering wings of birds
gone mad or astray. Sometimes though they come
out of my belly button, they cluster along
the slope of my shoulders, they roll right off
the tip of my tongue, after a slow crawl
through desire and fear. They remember
wild hands that strangled a song in my throat.
I floated like a movie star to another angle
to see if what I knew was happening. I lost
an earring, the wail in my mouth. I heard
the way my father's lips sneaked up above
his teeth, caressed the silver wings
of his partial plate, its too pink gums.
They made a zipper's hissing sound.
I was afraid, I had terrified hands, I
was sorrowful. Over his shoulder I noticed
the kitchen table was not clean.

Bird of Silence

It's great when the ancestors visit.
But when I try to take them into a crowd
they lose me, they leave me there, their
small voices become a low whisper. So
I can get to screaming with rage,
not meaning to. Not rage. It's more
desperate, urgent with light.

Some of the white girls tell me to shove it.
The class girls, you know what I mean. I say
shove it, really, they say lower your voice,
their pale hands measuring the air
like they own it. They're no blood relation
to me, my mother once said about my father,
and his side, the Sicilians. She was driving.
She screamed with rage unfamiliar to us both.
Her fist pounded and pounded the steering wheel,
she blazed with her anger. I lost her, I knew it.
To die for, I say some days, of the memories.

Silly Bird, I Love You

You're my favorite. Better than
the ponies of dreaming, you fly
up unexpected. What I love best
is your wild mouth, the way songs
come out of your throat all cockeyed
and toothless. I'm laughing now.
Remember the way we love water? Still do.
It's mostly at seashore or lakeside
you find me. The rest of the time
it's a memory I long for. Little bird,
favorite bird, silly bird, I'm listening
in the sorrow and rage, in the madness
all purple, even your small songs
are lovely. Early this morning
you began to hum in my ear, a lover's
tongue, my throat starts to quiver
and then I'm singing.

Hot Bird of Longing

Ooh I said

you just gave me a little sexual thrill
and oops I went hot through the middle
of lust again. It was morning near
the sea, early for unusual lust. I love
losing in moments of bliss, even alone.
Up the throat roams desire, the sea
is so large. You say you remember
once loving the dress that I wore,
the last time we danced all alone
in the woods, you called me dear.
Once you leaped over the bar
in your tux shirt, hot butch that you are,
and desire swam through me for hours.
Once you held lemons and limes
in the olive-skinned bowl of your hands,
long fingers caressing them whole, lovely,
you loved how I wanted you, so easy,
dark eyes, gold chains round your neck
all shiny. I call you, recall you.

Crying Bird

Even the birds cry, Mamma. Across
species I hear the same old longing:
Come home, come home, this is our life,
oh Mamma, oh baby. I remember coarse
whispers, rising in the night to see
you crying in the kitchen, back door
open to stars, the sound of the car,
leaving. By ourselves, Mamma, we could
have made it, it's still what I long for
alone in my forties. Not a child, but
to be yours again, the old ways we danced,
your palm tender on my cheek, the small
phrases you'd whisper, our secrets. Too
many years without you have made me come
loose from your treasure. Out here
on the sea I recall it and weep. I
think I've gone hard, Mamma, tough bird
in salt air. I think I've grown old,
Mamma, old to our longing. I'm rocking
and swaying in storm. I open my palms,
my mouth, welcoming the rain. I sing
a small song, it's full of blue air,
the same as our sorrow, what's left us
behind. If I return to my longing
what I might find in an infant of sorrow,
departure, or worse, left loose in the sea,
all alone, full of rage.

Bird of the Lake

Even in paradise small birds are homeless.
Over tea at the lake one fell from a tree
squawking with rage. It could have been
sorrow, desperate, madness. I fled back
and away from its rage, a mother offered
her finger till it landed and stayed,
its beak pointy, glaring. I
was afraid of its yelling, the blaze
in its eyes. *Disease* I thought
or *dying*. They're coming in waves.

Get real. A bird fell outada fuckin' tree.
That's it. So make a big deal of it,
be a poet again, go preen your feathers
in front of the angels. Ha Ha.
He says, the voice of his memory says.

My ancestors' wings belong to their shoulders.
No angels or demons prance around, ridiculous.
They won't use the time, Sicilians, Calabrians,
wiseguys and hardheads. Stubborn, they lug
their burdens around for years.

They were poor, a white man said once, sure
of himself, grinning. They had no clothes.
They were dirty, they plunged their dirty
hands right into the bowls of spaghetti
set out on the table and ate, using
the raggedy skirts of the women to wipe

red sauce from their mouths.
They are some of the women who tell me
to say so, but mostly in dreams: a bowl
of hands, a bowl of seashell, a bowl
of time full of rivers and sky. If
I try to stay quiet I ache so, low
in my back, or the center of longing.
Their voices yell below my heart,
'pay attention to us,' they are screaming,
'we love you.'

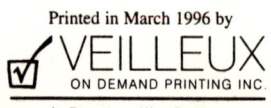

Printed in March 1996 by
VEILLEUX
ON DEMAND PRINTING INC.
in Boucherville, Quebec